THE MONOTYPES OF JOSEPH SOLMAN

[OVERLEAF] 1. DUNES AND BEACH. 1971. 10 X 14

The Monotypes of Joseph Solman

INTRODUCTION BY *Una E. Johnson* CURATOR EMERITUS, THE BROOKLYN MUSEUM

WITH TECHNICAL NOTES BY THE ARTIST ON THE MAKING OF THE PRINTS

Da Capo Press · New York · 1977

Library of Congress Cataloging in Publication Data

Solman, Joseph, 1909-
   The monotypes of Joseph Solman.

   Bibliography: p.
   1. Solman, Joseph, 1909-   2. Monotype
(Engraving)—Technique. I. Title.
NE2246.S64A5   769'.92'4   77-9923
ISBN 0-306-77425-9

Published by Da Capo Press, Inc.
A Subsidiary of Plenum Publishing Corporation
227 West 17th Street, New York, N.Y. 10011

Designed by Abe Lerner

To Ruth

INTRODUCTION

SIMILAR to many American artists whose professional careers began during the early years of the 1930s, Joseph Solman continued to develop his abilities as a painter on the Federal Arts Project of the Works Progress Administration in New York City. Solman's early paintings came to the notice of a few critics and art dealers in the mid–1930s. His manner of painting was in an expressionist idiom rather than that of social comment or regionalism. His visual interests led him to seek out paintings by artists who were following the mainstream of modern art. At this time only a few galleries in New York were promoting the works of more venturesome artists. Among those whose paintings were exhibited were Alfred Maurer, John Marin, Max Weber, and also the paintings of Stuart Davis, Marsden Hartley, Karl Knaths and Milton Avery. This left a large number of young artists with only occasional representation in group exhibitions. It was in such a frustrating atmosphere that a group of artists known as *The Ten* was formed. Their initial meeting was held in Solman's studio located at 15th Street and Second Avenue in New York. Among those attending this meeting were Ben-Zion, Ilya Bolotowsky, Adolph Gottlieb, Mark Rothko, Louis Schanker and Joseph Solman. Later *The Ten* was joined by John Graham, Earl Kerkam and Ralph Rosenborg. A loosely knit group, they were bound by no particular style but were fully united in their rebellion against a sentimental romanticism and an American regionalism that they believed to be the prevailing manner of painting. Their first exhibition was held at the Montross Gallery on Fifth Avenue in December 1935. Their works revealed a number of styles including formal abstraction, a tentative cubism that veiled a figurative structure, and a simplified expressionism. Beginning in 1935 *The Ten* took full advantage of the experimentation and consultation with other artists offered by the Federal Arts Project.

Joseph Brummer, a highly respected art dealer, was invited to see their first exhibition. He admired their aggressive point of view and suggested they plan a European showing of their paintings. He also arranged for the exhibition at the Galerie Bonaparte in Paris and defrayed all expenses. Opening in November 1936, the exhibition created considerable attention among the French critics who were intrigued with this new, robust direction in American painting. In New York *The Ten* soon held a second exhibition at the Montross Gallery. They were determined to carry on their thrusts against what they called American academic painting and against a stultifying regionalism. Gradually their efforts were noticed and the individual artists of the group began to gain recognition. By 1940 a number of them were located in various New York galleries and, by mutual consent, they ceased to function as a group. Perhaps their most positive accomplishment was the active demonstration of the growing vigor, diversity and independence of American painting. Soon each artist found his own particular *metier* in pure abstraction, in poetic realism, in a low-keyed expressionism, or in abstract expressionism.

Joseph Solman has held to a very personal style based on his own vision of realism and the drama of flattened and compressed expressionism. His ability to give inanimate objects or images a pulsating life of their own is present in his provocative compositions that reveal unpretentious visions of city streets and interiors. These easel size paintings, devoid of human figures, are full of an inner presence and understated mystery. His intent is to capture a mood of isolation through the casual drama of signs, symbols, and crude letters that appear on an otherwise undistinguished city street. His interest is caught by the clutter of objects on a table or bench where the sudden yellow of reflected light streams through a mullioned window. The obsolete tar carts that formerly were pulled around city streets behind the trucks of repair crews take on a strange, nostalgic abandonment. Their muted blacks, blues, reds and yellows lend them an awkward grace.

Solman's response to those who question the lack of figures in his paintings is that a city street or an interior contain much more pictorial drama when they are stripped of extraneous or disruptive factors. He quotes Delacroix's observations on still life painting: "What a strange thing painting is, pleasing us by its resemblance to objects that could not please us by themselves." Solman reserves his figurative work for his many distinguished portraits that have been recognized by collectors and critics alike. With great attention to the development of his chosen design or image as well as to background areas Solman well understands that every part of his composition must fall into its proper and logical place. From his *Portrait of Eddie,* a race track character, to his studio interiors and city streets, the artist's sensibility to the mood or character of his subject is always evident.

In 1942 during the time of an exhibition of Solman's paintings, the well-known museum director Duncan Phillips acquired several of the artist's canvasses. Nearly a decade later, in 1949, a large exhibition of Solman's work was held at the Phillips Memorial Gallery in Washington, D.C. Subsequently Duncan Phillips added other Solman paintings to his collection. Solman continued to pursue his visual explorations, intent on refining and illuminating the essence of a character and the special profiles of objects in a studio interior.

Solman began extensive experiments in the art of the monotype in June of 1968 after he and his wife had acquired a studio and summer home on Cape Ann. He brought with him a great sheaf of drawings that would serve as the fundamental part of his new venture. Although he was familiar with the fine monotypes of Edgar Degas, this was Solman's first serious effort in the realm of the printed image. In 1944 he had worked briefly in silk screen under the guidance of Leonard Pytlak and had composed a series of studies for a portrait of Mozart. But he preferred a more direct and personal method of working. Solman had been greatly impressed with the watercolors and drawings of Paul Klee and, over a number of years, acquired a few of Klee's drawings. He was fascinated by the simplicity and the taut, vibrating qualities of line that characterize Klee's most eloquent compositions. Klee often combined a number of techniques to achieve his desired images. Solman surmised that the unusual texture of the lines that gave Klee's compositions refinement and sense of mystery was due, in part, to this artist's application of a form of monotype printing.

Artists have found in the monotype a medium that is closely akin to painting. It is a free and immediate means of obtaining a colorful printed image without the necessity of carrying out the technical demands of etching, engraving or lithography. It is also a medium that allows the artist entire control of the work itself. All that is basically required is a smooth, rigid surface—a piece of glass or a metal sheet—on which to paint in oil, watercolor or printer's inks the desired image. The final step is to transfer that image to a sheet of paper by means of an etching press or, in Solman's case, by hand or spoon pressure.

The monotype was invented by an Italian artist, Benedetto Castiglione, who lived in Genoa in the seventeenth century. However, little was done to further its development until the innovations of William Blake in England and later in France where Degas, Gauguin, Rouault and others found it a most sympathetic and rewarding medium. Paul Klee, Max Ernst and Jean Dubuffet also found the monotype and its unpredictable imagery much to their liking. In United States outstanding results in the medium were achieved by Maurice Prendergast, Eugene Higgins, John Sloan, Pop Hart, Milton Avery and Abraham Walkowitz. Still later the monotype was successfully employed with numerous variations by Bertoia, Morris Graves, Boris Margo, Adja Yunkers and others. The very nature of the monotype demands both the skills of a draftsman and those of a painter. It permits a single printed impression with a possible second but much less distinct image. Each new print must be an immediate success or failure because there is no margin for error or change. Solman observes that a failure has but one destination— the waste paper basket. Nevertheless this tantalizing risk often results in unforeseen subtleties in color and in composition.

For the past ten summers Joseph Solman has been engaged in developing his own approaches to the monotype print. The delightful series of his favored composition, the tar cart, appears in his early prints. As in his drawings and paintings the carts stand on rickety wheels, their lines diffused and their form heavily massed in a single expressive image. Deftly placed on an otherwise blank sheet of white paper this arresting and unusual image conveys a sense of abandonment and mystery (pls. 2 & 3). The skillful employment of changing textures and quivering or vibrating lines give variety and liveliness to Solman's compositions. To the artist, back-

ground areas are as important as the image itself and lend color, balance and coherence to his basic concept. In some of his beach scenes the figures, set against a high horizon, are denoted by small, calligraphic strokes of a brush (pl. 17). In others a table and two unoccupied chairs are placed against a suggested lawn (pl. 12). A seated nude figure denoted by a single moving line is set against a lightly patterned background (pl. 7). A cluster of trees is given a low-keyed intensity through careful handling of textured masses and strong light lines (pl. 28).

Unusual or generally ignored objects have always had a special appeal for Solman. He has sought to impart a particular mood or arrested motion in his monotypes of a cradled telephone or a pair of eyeglasses resting on a white background. Last summer while rummaging through a small antique shop on Cape Ann the artist found an old camera, its bellows long since exhausted and its mechanism lost. Acquiring this object, Solman set it up in his studio as a still life composition. Mixing many colors into a mauve image on his glass plate and accenting or wiping out certain areas or outlines he quickly printed this elusive image. He insists it was a happy accident. Its antique, subdued tones and its nearly forgotten imagery seem to recall the earlier art of the daguerreotype.

More recently Solman has become interested in the complex designs of parked motorcycles. Their heavy wheels, the sudden angles of the protruding handlebars and the embellishments of mirrors and luggage racks appear to the artist as further symbols of a city street. Unlike his nostalgic tar carts, the image of the motorcycle evokes a sense of restrained power, speed and sound. In this latest series of monotypes the artist demonstrates anew his ability to suggest and amplify through visual means the hidden elements he perceives in a specific inanimate object.

Solman's personal contributions to the art of the monotype lie in his development and control of vibrating or quivering lines, his presentation of objects or forms in sharp edged or shaved–off masses, and in his freedom in the application of white or slightly toned backgrounds. His monotypes as well as his drawings and paintings are forged in the expressionist tradition. Nevertheless, the artist believes that recognizable images also have many qualities of abstraction in the extended ideas and concepts they may evoke. During the past ten years Joseph Solman has issued more than five hundred monotypes of varying simplicity or complexity. They amply record the artist's visual sensibilities and his engaging involvement with the signs and symbols of his time.

UNA E. JOHNSON
Curator Emeritus, The Brooklyn Museum

The Monotypes

2. RUSTY TAR CART. 1974. 10 X 14. COLLECTION ABE LERNER

3. PAIL AND CART. 1973. 10½ X 12

4. LAWN WITH STROLLER. 1970. 11 X 14. COLLECTION JOSEPH HIRSHHORN

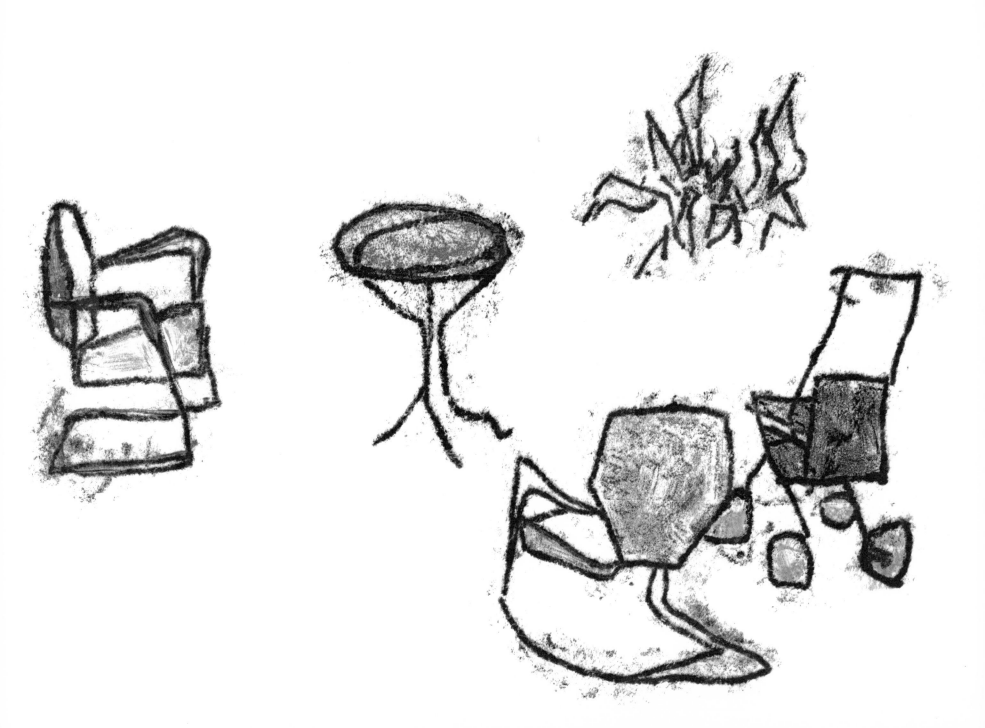

5. TWO MOTORCYCLES. 1975. 11½ x 14½

6. PARKED MOTORCYCLE. 1975. 10½ x 14

7. CROUCHING FIGURE. 1974. 11 X 15. COLLECTION MR. AND MRS. BLACKBURN

Joseph Solman '74

8. FIRE WAGON I. 1973. 11 X 13

9. TAR CART I. 1968. 10½ x 16. COLLECTION MR. AND MRS. SYD WEISS

10. THE GERANIUM PLANT. 1975. 10½ x 14

Joseph Solman '75

11. LAWN CHAIRS. 1973. 9 X 12

12. LAWN. 1970. 8½ x 10½

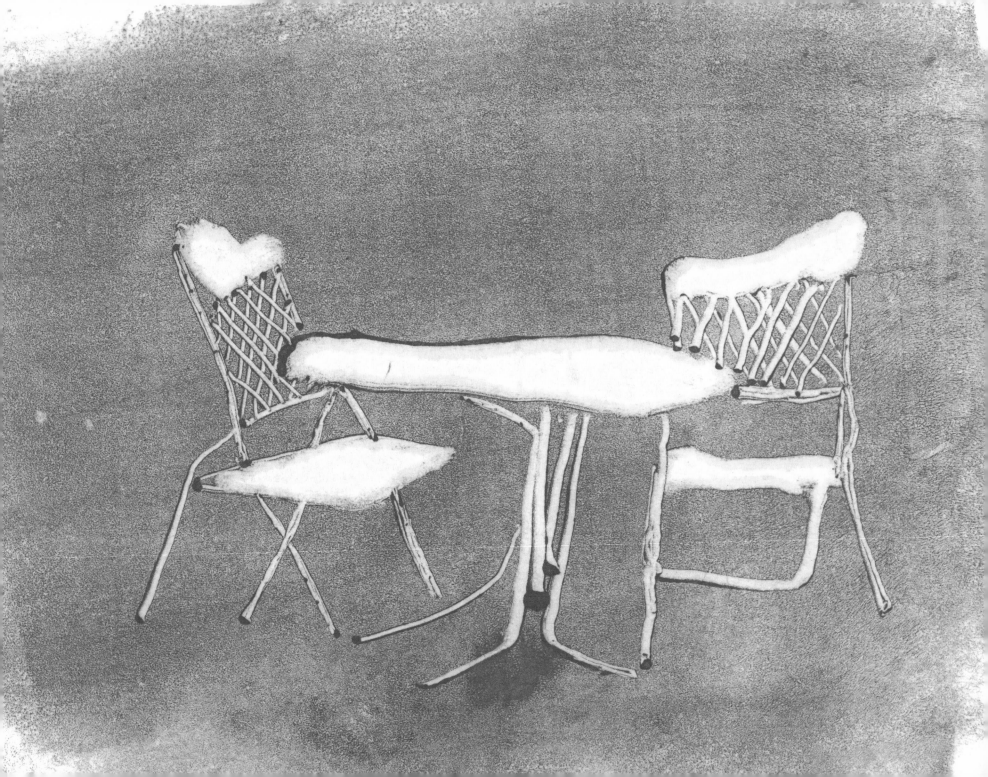

13. KITCHEN SCENE. 1970. 10 x 14. NATIONAL COLLECTION OF FINE ARTS, WASH. D.C.

JS

14. STUDIO INTERIOR. 1969. 11 X 14. COLLECTION DR. AND MRS. JULES RUBIN

15. NUDE. 1970. 11 X 14½

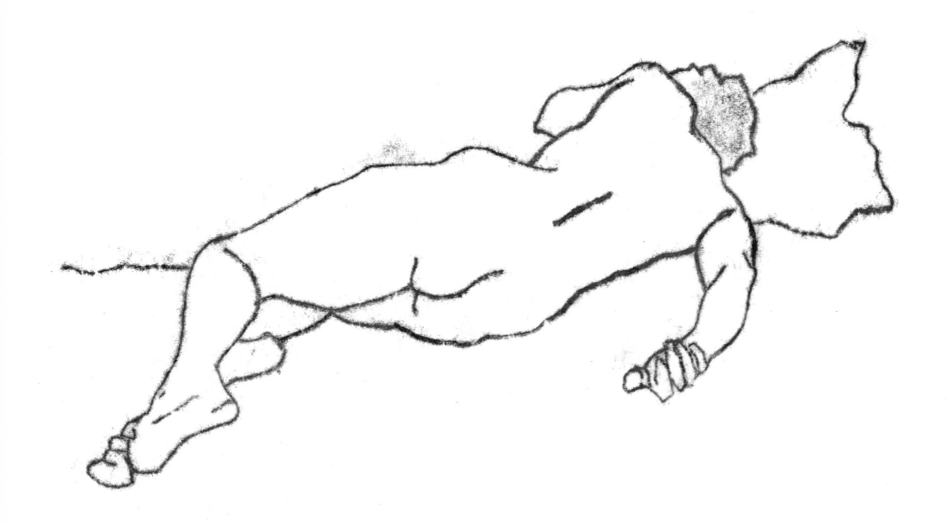

16. DAY'S END. 1969. 12·X 14

17. GOOD HARBOR BEACH. 1973. 9½ X 12

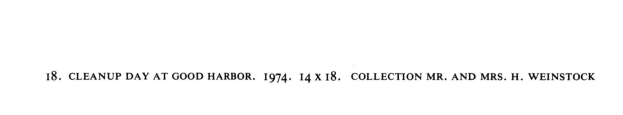

18. CLEANUP DAY AT GOOD HARBOR. 1974. 14 X 18. COLLECTION MR. AND MRS. H. WEINSTOCK

19. TRUCK AT BEACH. 1975. 14 X 16½

20. BLUE TRUCK. 1974. 10 X 13

21. MOTORCYCLE. 1975. 12 X 15½. COLLECTION MRS. MIRIAM BEGG

22. TRIO. 1974. 8 x 11. COLLECTION ARTIST'S WIFE

23. PARKED. 1976. 14 x 18

24. HONDA BY THE SEA. 1975. 11 X 14

25. BMW. 1976. 14 X 10

26. THE GANG. 1976. 12 X 16

27. LEAVES. 1975. 17 X 13

28. A GYRE OF TREES. 1974. 13 X 17

29. ROCK AND TREES. 1970. II X 9. COLLECTION JOHN SIMON

30. TREES IN GLOUCESTER. 1974. 11½ x 16½

Joseph Solman

31. MARSHES AND SEA. 1976. 11½ X 17. COLLECTION MR. AND MRS. FRANK DONNOLA

32. TREES ON WITHAM STREET. 1974. 12½ x 18

33. PAUL ROBINSON. 1971. 13 X 11

34. GRAPHLEX. 1976. 10 X 14

35. OLD CAMERA. 1975. 10 X 11. COLLECTION ABE LERNER

36. CAMERA. 1975. 10 X 14

37. MA BELL. 1976. 10½ x 14½

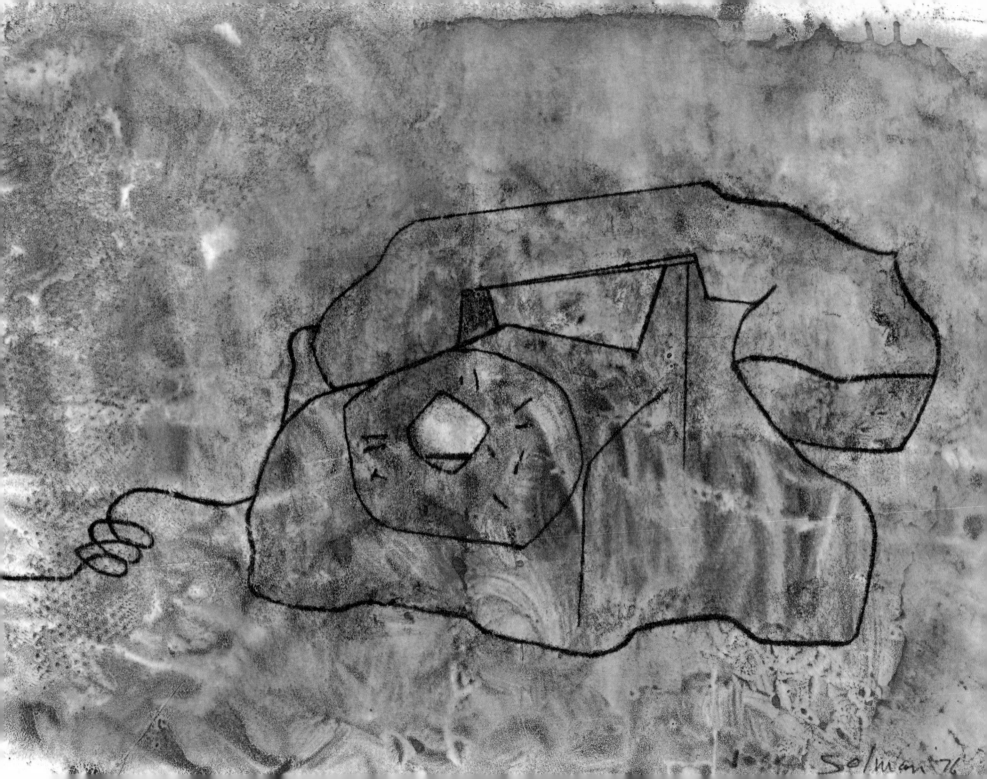

Solman 76

38. FIRE WAGON II. 1974. 10 X 17. COLLECTION MR. AND MRS. BARRY GERSON

39. TAR CART II. 1973. 11 X 12

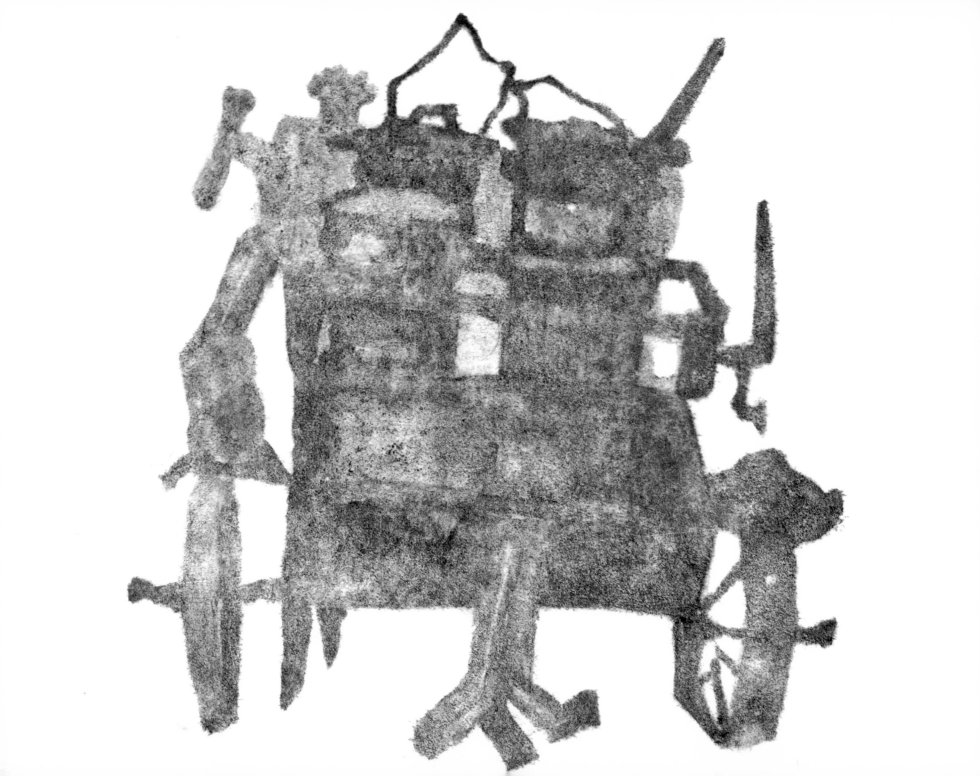

40. TAR CART PROFILE. 1969. 11 X 16. COLLECTION PAUL SOLMAN

Joseph Solman

41. FIRE WAGON III. 1974. 9½ x 15

Joseph Solman '74

MONOTYPE AND METHODS *by JOSEPH SOLMAN*

A MONOTYPE is a single, printed impression produced by painting a picture or design on a flat surface of glass or metal, and transferring it onto a sheet of paper by means of pressure. The methods of pressure vary from rubbing by hand or spoon to a heavy roller or etching press. In effect the monotype combines the spontaneous quality of a drawing, wash or oil sketch with the "magical" impress of a fine print, leaving the artist a spectator, so to speak, at its birth. The word *monotype* is used because the one transfer that is generally made removes most of the paint or ink from the surface of the plate.[1]

The painting medium is usually oil thinned with turpentine, but printers' ink or watercolor are also favored. Japan rice paper is preferred because of its excellent absorbent quality but fine-grained watercolor paper may be equally effective.

If the monotype medium limits the artist to a single print in contrast to the multiple impressions possible in etching or lithography, why should not the artist paint his picture directly on the paper in the first place? Henry Rasmusen, artist and author of *Printmaking With Monotype*[2], gives this answer: "For textural variety, surface quality and subtlety of coloration, there is no other medium that can approach the monotype. It is a means of creative invention, surprises, excitement, spontaneity and organic rightness. Between the original painting on the plate and the finished impression there often takes place a transformation of the mundane into the magical."

The fact that practically no two monotypists use exactly the same methods is illustrative of the extensive possibilities for personal expression in the medium. Among the various techniques I have explored are:

MONOTYPE LINE-TRANSFER

This simple method involves placing the drawing or design under the glass, making registration marks at the two lower points of the paper. Then stipple or brush oil colors with a flat bristle brush on the glass, covering broadly all the linear areas of the drawing that you see through the glass—with varied hues and colors or simply in monochrome. After the paint is surface dry in an hour or two (testing it gently for excess paint with flat sheets of newspaper), place the printing paper on the glass, mask-taping the top ends to the glass. The glass should be hinged to a box or board so it can be lifted up or down. Pull drawing out from under glass. Now place the drawing face up on *top* of the rice paper in the same position it occupied under the glass, taping its top two ends to the rice paper. Using a hard rounded point, like the opposite end of a small lobster fork, a pencil or stylus, trace your drawing freely or closely with

[1] A second transfer is usually faint though Degas often used this lighter proof as a ground for building up his pastel studies.

[2] *Printmaking With Monotype* by Henry Rasmusen and published by Chilton Co. (Philadelphia and New York) is the only comprehensive book on the history and various printing techniques of monotype. It is unfortunately out of print.

sharp and even pressure. This will transfer the paint on the glass onto the print paper precisely where you have pressed the tool. Disengage with care both drawing and print from glass. This is called a linear transfer monotype and is typical of the frontispiece and nudes.

LINE-TRANSFER OVER COLORED GROUND

This is a more involved variant of the above method. Float a colored background on top of the glass, thinning the paint liberally with turpentine and then placing the print paper over the glass in this wet state, pressing the entire area of the paper with your palm. Tape the top of this paper to top of glass to enable you to flap paper gently back away from glass. Wipe glass clean with turps and cloth. Now stipple areas of oil color as described in previous example. Wait and test for drying process. Pull drawing out from under glass, then flap print paper back onto glass. Pinpoint and tape drawing on top of print paper in the same position it occupied under the glass and trace with some tool (even the end of a paint brush will do) those lines you want transferred to already colored background. Plates 25 and 41 are examples of this method.

MASSED OR SILHOUETTE SHAPES BY MEANS OF WIPE-OUT

Still another variant is to cover the entire areas of the design in the usual stipple brush manner. Use tones and colors relating to the final picture you have in mind. After surface drying, place print paper on glass and then the drawing on top of print paper and trace sharply to achieve a line transfer. Remove print and drawing. On the painted glass the pressure of the tracing tool will show light negative lines like a fossilized imprint of whatever traceries you have made. Now using pieces of cloth, Q-tips or stiff pointed cardboard, remove or wipe away sections of the paint as though you were cutting areas of wood away similar to a woodcut design, using the light lines on your glass as guide or boundary. When ultimately pleased

with whatever design you choose to leave on the glass, lightly swab a fresh piece of print paper with turpentine or kerosene, using a clean flat kitchen sponge. Place paper on glass and tape firmly at top. Put a sheet of any paper over the print paper to prevent tearing, then rub over entire area with back of large salad spoon, barin or wooden spatula, checking intermittently how the transfer is taking by lifting print paper up gently but not past the masking tape. Continue rubbing till satisfied with resultant transfer or monotype. Some silhouette-like images are examples of this method. See Pl. 18.

It was Giovanni Benedetto Castiglione who in 1635 first developed the idea of a monotype painting. After noting how different in tone his etching proofs were, he decided to cover a copperplate with printing ink and create a design by wiping into the inked surface with a brush, rag, stick or even his fingers. This procedure consists of creating highlights, of working from dark to light. The plate, covered with a sheet of damp paper, is then run through the etching press and the design is transferred from plate to paper.

Degas practically reinvented this method in 1876 with some help from a fellow etcher Lepic. He worked intermittently with the medium till 1893 and, through his genius, lifted it into the realm of art as another important vehicle of the artist's expression. The method of the gradual wipeout is generally called the "dark field" manner or the subtractive method. Degas also worked in the "light field" manner, which is the direct application of ink or color to a clean plate with a brush and sometimes a cloth to clean or vary tones.

The larger number of monotypes made by Gauguin were, in reality, transfer drawings. In a letter of 1902 to Gustave Fayet, Gauguin wrote: "First you roll out printer's ink on a sheet of paper of any sort; then lay a second sheet on top of it and draw whatever pleases you. The harder and thinner your pencil, the finer will be the resulting line." Gauguin, by further pressing the surface of the drawing with his fingers, a spoon or a piece of cardboard, created a play of tone and a mysterious chiaroscuro to enhance the monotype. Gauguin used many of these "trace monotypes" as studies for his paintings.

Richard S. Feld, in his introduction to *Gauguin: The Monotypes,* makes this fine summation: "The monotype permitted the artist to make endless and somewhat unpredictable variations on the drawings he had saved from previous years. . . . Begun as a cheap and easy method for the duplication of drawings, the monotype all but replaced charcoal and pencil drawing the last four years of Gauguin's life. . . . In essence, the monotype permitted the grafting of new ideas to older forms."

Gauguin also made about thirty-five watercolor monotypes by simply transferring a wet watercolor from one sheet of paper to another to obtain a more diffuse and poetic effect.

Hardly any but a handful of artists realize that Paul Klee made hundreds of monotypes, usually tracing the medium over or under his watercolors and gesso grounds, notably in his work of the twenties. Hans Moller, the fine landscape painter who experimented in Klee's technique some years ago, wrote me the following: "Klee rolled black printer's ink on glass or stone, placed his paper on the stiff surface and drew on the back of the paper with pencil or stylus or even his fingernails. One can see in many instances the finger-marks where he held down or pressed the paper. He probably built up his intricate watercolor tints over the transfer drawing since the greasy black ink is repellent to watercolor. . . ."

Klee also used the traced-design process, somewhat like Gauguin, in many so-called oil drawings. In this manner his wayward line was susceptible of incorporating accidents, variations of intensity, interruptions, and vibrations. It was Klee's work in this form that was my magnet to the medium.

The subtle radiance of Maurice Prendergast's monotypes places him at the peak of the American practitioners of the medium. He explored the monotype in the form of a personal impressionism and intimate arrangement of clusters of women and children: on beaches and bridges, in parks and circuses. He created, single-handedly, an exquisite order in an otherwise fluid medium.

Abraham Walkowitz executed a number of monotypes in black and white and in sepia, particularly a series of touching Lower East Side figures and groups of bathers, weighty and simple. There is a charm, a naiveté, a sort of awkward grace in his figures.

Eugene Higgins devoted a large part of his creative career to printing monochromatic monotypes by means of his etching press. They exhibit a mysterious, yet earthy poetry. Higgins deserves some research to restore him to his rightful place in the sphere of this medium.

Done on glass, printed by hand, usually on rice or watercolor paper, Milton Avery's monotypes project simplified, monumental forms done with his typical fresh wit and spontaneity. He utilized scratching, saturation with turpentine or water, stick and brushwork and overpainting for his bold and adventurous work in this medium.

Will Barnet, experimenting with the monotype in the mid–1930s, poured thick mineral oil on his copperplate before painting on it in oil and then printing by press. He was also the subject of a film on how to make a monotype during the same period.

Matt Phillips, a veteran practitioner of the monotype, applies dry brush strokes into a wet surface, scratching with the end of the brush, and wiping parts of the surface with a cloth to obtain varied whites on the final print. He uses a press for large prints and a common spoon for smaller ones. Phillips refers to the plate as an "arena of quicksilver activity, always fluid, open to change and risk, like playing jazz; the image being built or cancelled out by a cloth wipe or turpentine."

Among some earlier practitioners, Frank Duveneck, William Chase, and John Sloan deserve more space than I can spare. And among contemporaries, veterans of the medium like Mary Frank and Nathan Oliviera may be mentioned as well as Boris Margo, Hedda Sterne, Adja Yunkers, Herman Rose, Leon Goldin, Richard Mills, and many more.

Chronology

First one-man exhibition at Contemporary Arts Gallery, N.Y.C., 1934.

Formed group called *The Ten* with Rothko, Bolotowsky, Gottlieb, Ben-Zion, Kerkam, Schanker and others, 1936.

Editor–in–chief of *Art Front Magazine,* 1937-38.

Three-man show with Gromaire and Rothko at New Art Circle, 1940.

Retrospective of paintings at Phillips Gallery, Washington, D.C., 1949.

Joined A.C.A. Gallery, 1952.

Instructor of painting at Museum of Modern Art, 1952-54.

International Association of Plastic Arts travelling show of 75 contemporary Americans throughout Europe, 1956-57.

National Institute of Arts and Letters award for painting, 1961.

President of Federation of Modern Painters and Sculptors, 1965-67.

First exhibition of monotypes at Herbert E. Feist Gallery, 1969.

Instructor of painting and drawing at C.C.N.Y., 1967-75.

Saltus Gold Medal and Ranger Fund Purchase of oil at National Academy of Design, 1971.

Childe Hassam Awards, 1969 and 1972.

Maynard and Neilson portrait awards at National Academy, 1975 and 1976.

Bibliography

Burray, S. "Solman: The Growth of Conviction." *Arts Magazine,* October, 1955.

Joseph Solman (148 plates, including 16 in full color) with an Introduction by A. L. Chanin, Docent, Museum of Modern Art. Crown Publishers Inc., New York, 1966.

Medoff, Eve. "Joseph Solman, a Forty Year Retrospective." *American Artist,* November, 1973.

Schramm, Jean. "Solman's New York." *American Arts Monthly,* 1935.

Seckler, Dorothy. "Problems of Portraiture." *Art in America,* Winter, 1958-59.

Seckler, Dorothy. "Solman Paints a Picture." *Art News,* Summer, 1951.

Solman, Joseph. "The Easel Division." *The New Deal Art Projects; An Anthology of Memoirs,* 1972.

The monotypes of Joseph Solman are in the following museums: National Collection of Fine Arts, Washington, D.C.; The Joseph Hirshhorn Museum, Washington, D.C.; The Fogg Museum, Cambridge, Massachusetts; Yale University Museum, New Haven, Connecticut; Los Angeles County Museum, Los Angeles, California; E. A. Ulrich Museum, Wichita, Kansas; and in several private collections.